PLANTING

WITH
PERENNIALS

Richard Bird

An imprint of Anness Publishing Ltd, Hermes House, 88–89 Blackfriars Road London SE1 8HA; tel. 020 7401 2077; fax 020 7633 9499; www.annesspublishing.com

If you like the images in this book and would like to investigate using them for publishing, promotions or advertising, please visit our website www.practicalpictures.com for more information.

Publisher: Joanna Lorenz
Managing Editor: Helen Sudell
Editor: Valerie Ferguson
Series Designer: Larraine Shamwana
Designer: Andrew Heath
Editorial Reader: Richard McGinlay
Production Controller: Joanna King
Photography: Peter Anderson, Jonathan Buckley, John Freeman, Michelle Garrett, Andrea Jones, Simon McBride

ETHICAL TRADING POLICY

At Anness Publishing we believe that business should be conducted in an ethical and ecologically sustainable way, with respect for the environment and a proper regard to the replacement of the natural resources we employ. We are therefore currently growing more than 750,000 trees in three Scottish forest plantations.
Because of this ongoing ecological investment programme, you, as our customer, can have the pleasure and reassurance of knowing that a tree is being cultivated on your behalf to naturally replace the materials used to make the book you are holding.
For further information about this scheme, go to www.annesspublishing.com/trees

NOTES

For all recipes, quantities are given in both metric and imperial measures and, where appropriate, in standard cups and spoons. Follow one set of measures, but not a mixture, because they are not interchangeable.
Standard spoon and cup measures are level. 1 tsp = 5ml, 1 tbsp = 15ml, 1 cup = 250ml/8fl oz. Australian standard tablespoons are 20ml. Australian readers should use 3 tsp in place of 1 tbsp for measuring small quantities.
American pints are 16fl oz/2 cups. American readers should use 20fl oz/2.5 cups in place of 1 pint when measuring liquids.
Electric oven temperatures in this book are for conventional ovens. When using a fan oven, the temperature will probably need to be reduced by about 10–20°C/20–40°F. Since ovens vary, you should check with your manufacturer's instruction book for guidance. Medium (US large) eggs are used unless otherwise stated.

PUBLISHER'S NOTE: Although the advice and information in this book are believed to be accurate and true at the time of going to press, neither the authors nor the publisher can accept any legal responsibility or liability for any errors or omissions that may be made.

CONTENTS

Introduction

PERENNIALS ARE REGAINING THEIR POPULARITY AT THE FOREFRONT OF GARDENING. WHILE SHRUBS PROVIDE THE BASIC STRUCTURE OF A BORDER AND ANNUALS TEMPORARY COLOUR, PERENNIALS FORM THE PERMANENT PLANTINGS THAT CREATE THE MAIN INTEREST.

WHAT IS A PERENNIAL?

In theory, perennials are plants that live more than one or two years. However, in gardening terms there are certain perennials that fit this definition but are not generally included in this category: woody plants, such as trees and shrubs, for example. Within this group some sub-shrubs, including *Dianthus* and *Perovskia*, are usually

Above: Perennials are suitable for any garden style, such as this lush planting.

included as perennials. Alpines, most of which are perennials, are also often considered as a separate category. Bulbs are usually excluded as a group but individuals such as lilies are included. Many perennials are herbaceous plants in that they die back each year below ground and reappear in spring, but there are also those, some irises for example, that wholly or in part remain evergreen throughout the winter.

WHY CHOOSE PERENNIALS?

Perennials form the backbone of a garden, adding a wealth of colour, shape and texture. They have the advantage over annuals in that they reappear every year, basically recreating the same border, so that you do not have to worry about the overall picture each year, just the detail. Their versatility is astonishing, as there are plants for every type of garden situation as well as for every style and type of border design. No matter whether you live in the countryside, by the sea or in the middle of town, you will find that there are ample perennials to suit all your needs.

HOW TO CHOOSE PERENNIALS

As when choosing any other garden plants, it is important to consider the physical environment in which you live: the type of soil, whether it is moist or dry, whether it is in sun or shade or exposed to winds. Generally this will limit your choice of plants to some degree but there will still be plenty to choose from. The design is a much more personal matter: deciding which plants will create the look you want. It is important at this stage to consider the colour, shape and texture of not only the flowers but also the foliage and overall planting to obtain the most pleasing effect.

Above: The contrasting shapes of perennials give the gardener plenty of scope for designing interesting and dynamic borders.

Above: This classic mixed border of spring-flowering perennials contains a wonderful mixture of fresh, bright colours.

Introduction

SELECTING HEALTHY PLANTS

From the maintenance point of view it is important to select only plants that are healthy and strong. Some perennials are very tough, in terms of resisting both the weather and disease. These are not necessarily unattractive plants, many having come down to us through cottage gardens, and are always worth considering for a trouble-free garden. Many of the modern cultivars are more brightly coloured and have larger flowers but have not got the same resistance, so select your plants or seeds with care. It is always useful to look at other gardens in your area: plants that are obviously thriving in your neighbours' gardens are also likely to do well for you.

Above: This border has a distinctive layered effect, with winter aconites in front of Helleborus foetidus.

THE IMPORTANCE OF FORM

The next aspect to consider is the look of the plant. There are innumerable permutations of colour, shape, texture and size, of both the flowers and the foliage. As we shall see in later chapters these must all be taken into consideration when combining plants together to form an attractive border. For example, however much you may like it, a tall red-flowered plant is no substitute where a short red one is required; you will either need to choose another plant, or change the design. It is always best to think about the design, and the function of the plants in the border, before you buy them. The texture and shape of the plant and its foliage are just as important as colour and size.

Above: There are many perennials, such as these primroses, that are robust and will thrive in most garden conditions.

Above: The tall spikes of stately Lythrum salicaria *provide a mass of mauve flowers in the summer. Plant them where they will be noticed.*

A Plant for All Seasons

Another important thing to remember about perennials is their flowering periods. Many only have a relatively short time in flower. This must be co-ordinated with other plants. You will be disappointed if you have two pink plants, that you hope will look stunning together, if one flowers in May and the other in September. Likewise, if you choose carefully the border can be full of colour throughout the growing season and often during the winter as well. Many plants also remain attractive when not in flower.

How to Use this Book

In this handbook you will find a comprehensive guide to successfully growing plants right through from the initial designs to the more complex business of propagation. *Perennials in the Garden* gives information on achieving different styles from formal to wildflower, how to create an attractive border in different locations and how to maintain it once it is established. An extensive section covers the use of colour in the garden and how different effects can be achieved. *Seasonal Splendour* shows you how to maintain interest in your garden throughout the year. The text is supported throughout by a wealth of inspirational pictures, as well as lists of plants that are suitable for any given situation. There is also a quick reference chart of recommended perennials with details about their requirements.

Above: Snapdragons are quite short and should be placed near the front of a border for maximum effect.

Getting Started with Perennials

MOST GARDENING TASKS ARE BASED ON COMMON SENSE, AND MANY VERY SUCCESSFUL GARDENERS HAVE LEARNT LARGELY BY TRIAL AND ERROR. WITH A LITTLE ADVICE, EVEN THE BEGINNER SHOULD FIND THAT GARDENING IS MUCH EASIER THAN THEY THOUGHT.

THE IMPORTANCE OF PREPARATION

Thorough preparation is the keystone to good gardening. If a border has been started off well then not only is the result better, but also the amount of time spent maintaining it is reduced dramatically. Removing all the weeds when the bed is empty is much easier than struggling to remove them once it is full of plants. Once constructed, beds of perennials tend to be left in situ for many years with only a few minor adjustments. There are two major aspects to the preparation. The first, as stated above, is removing the weeds and the second is conditioning the soil.

Above: New borders should be dug in the autumn and then raked over in spring to finish breaking down the soil.

GETTING RID OF WEEDS

The real problem weeds are the perennial weeds. Any piece left in the soil is likely to grow into a new weed and soon re-infest the bed, often becoming impossible to uproot without disturbing other plants. If your soil is light then most weeds can be removed as you dig, but if it is heavy the only real solution is to kill them off with a weedkiller, before you start to dig. If done properly this should be the only time you need to use chemicals. Other methods, such as smothering the weedy area with black plastic, are possible but you will need to wait a year

Above: Tall plants with deep roots, such as bronze fennel, prefer a well-dug soil that allows the roots to spread downwards.

and often longer before the toughest weeds are killed. The borders should be dug in the autumn and not planted until the following spring so that any remaining weed seeds have time to germinate and can be removed.

Above: Dig the ground to the full depth of a spade or fork and incorporate as much well-rotted organic material as possible.

Above: A thorough preparation will get the plants off to a good start and should provide you with a border that not only looks attractive but is also easy to maintain.

DIGGING

You should not attempt to dig the ground when it is waterlogged as this will harm the structure of the soil. Choose a time when the ground is firm but moist. Dig the ground deeply, at least to one spade's depth, not just below the surface. On heavier soils it will repay to double dig, to two spades' depth. Incorporate as much well-rotted organic material as possible, such as garden compost or farmyard manure. This will not only provide the plants with nutrients but the fibrous content will improve the texture, giving better drainage on heavy soils while making light soils more moisture-retentive.

9

OBTAINING PLANTS

There are several ways of obtaining perennial plants. Because most individual varieties are required in small quantities, usually in ones or threes, the most frequent method of obtaining plants is to buy them. If you want to propagate your own plants, it is best to do it by a vegetative means, such as by taking cuttings or by division, so as to be sure of the specific variety. Seed is not used so much for perennials as you cannot guarantee to get plants that are identical to the parent, and so it is only used where the precise colour is of little matter.

Buying Plants

It is best to buy from a reputable supplier. Plants bought from roadside stalls and doubtful nurseries may be cheaper but the labelling often leaves a lot to be desired and you cannot ensure that you are getting the plant you want. Never buy plants that look unhealthy. Anything with pests or diseased leaves, or plants that look drawn or pot-bound (the pot is full of clogged roots), should be avoided as they will create unnecessary work.

Plants from Cuttings

A large number of perennials can be raised from cuttings. These can be tip, stem or basal cuttings, depending on the variety. Tip cuttings are taken from the tip of non-flowering stems. Stem cuttings involve using other parts of the stem besides just the tip. Basal cuttings use the tips of the new growth that appears at the base of the plant, most frequently in spring but also at other times of year, especially if the plant is cut back to encourage new growth.

Above: Artemisia *will soon produce a mass of silvery foliage.*

Taking Cuttings

By following a few simple techniques you can multiply your plant stock at no cost.

1 Take cuttings from a healthy plant either as tip, stem or basal cuttings as here with this *Artemisia*. Place the cuttings immediately into a plastic bag to keep them fresh. Seal it and place it in a cool place out of the sun until required.

2 As soon as possible after cutting, trim off the base of the stem just beneath a node (leaf stalk), and trim off all the lower leaves, leaving one or two pairs at the tip of the cutting. Make all the cuts neat with no snags or loose pieces of material left on the cutting.

3 Fill a pot with good quality cutting compost (soil mix) and lightly press it down. Make a hole with a pencil or small dibber and insert the cutting almost up to the leaves. Firm the soil around the cutting so that there are no airholes around it. Some gardeners like to dip the prepared end of the cutting into a rooting hormone before planting, but most perennials root satisfactorily without this.

4 Gently water the pot, label it and place it in a plastic bag or into a propagator. Put in a warm, light place that is out of direct sunlight. When using a plastic bag make certain that the bag does not touch the foliage on the cutting. If condensation builds up on the inside of the bag, remove it, turn it inside out and replace it.

5 Some plants will root quickly; others may take a couple of months or more. Test regularly to see if roots have formed. Once the cuttings have produced a strong root system they can be removed from their pot and potted up individually into a good quality potting compost (soil mix).

PLANTS FROM DIVISION

Division is a simple process that will produce plants that are identical to the parent. It provides mature plants more quickly than by taking cuttings. It can only be performed on those plants with a rootstock that produces multiple growing points. It is not possible to do it for a plant with a single stem.

1 Dig up either the whole plant or a section of the plant that you want to divide. If the soil is dry, water thoroughly the day before.

2 Hold the plant and shake it. Much of the soil will drop off from the roots.

5 Insert each piece into a pot of good quality potting compost (soil mix). Firm down the compost and water thoroughly. Place in a shady position until it starts to grow away again.

3 As you shake and work, many plants will naturally fall into individual pieces. Sometimes slight persuasion is needed.

4 For heavier soils and plants with more tangled roots, shake and work the plant in a bucket of water. Again, many will fall apart, but some are more resistant and it will be necessary to cut into individual pieces, each with a growing point on it.

Above: Irises can become congested over time so will benefit from division. This should be done after flowering.

GROWING FROM SEED

As perennials grown from seed can vary in their flower and foliage colour as well as size, seed is only used for growing plants where variation is not a problem. In some plants, *Alchemilla mollis* for example, the differences will be so minute as not to matter, but in others, such as delphiniums, a wide variety of colours can be produced.

1 Fill a pot with a good quality sowing compost (soil mix) and gently press it down. Sow the seed thinly across the surface.

2 Cover the seeds with some fine gravel or grit. This will help to keep the surface moist as well as making it easier to water the seeds evenly. It also protects the vulnerable necks of the seedlings from rotting.

3 Label and water the pot. Hardy perennials do not need heat to germinate and the pots of seed can be placed outside in a shady place. However, if you want to speed up the process, place them in a propagator in a shaded greenhouse.

4 When the seedlings are large enough to handle they can be pricked out into individual pots. Hold the seedling by its leaves and not by the stem or root. Place in a cold frame or greenhouse until large enough to be moved outside. Acclimatize them in stages of an increasing number of hours per day, so that the plant becomes gradually hardened off to the outside conditions.

Above: Mimulus seed can be collected after flowering and either sown in pots or directly in the border.

Perennials Maintenance

An attractive bed depends very much on good maintenance. It should not need a great deal of attention, but some time spent on it will make all the difference. The general rule should be "little and often".

Watering and Feeding

If the bed has been prepared properly then there should be no need to feed or water during the year. Most gardeners try to grow plants that tolerate their indigenous conditions so that watering is not necessary. Well-rotted organic material dug into the ground and a mulch on top of it reduces moisture loss. It may be necessary to water newly planted areas until they are established if there are dry spells. Watering of whole borders is best done with a sprinkler, making certain that at least 3cm (1in) of water is delivered. Individual plants can be watered with a can, again making certain that the soil is properly soaked. Perennials in containers will also need watering. Containers, even large ones, dry out very quickly and they will need watering at least once a day in hot, dry weather.

Top-dressing a border with well-rotted organic material every winter or early spring should provide sufficient nutrients and no further feeding should be required except for plants in tubs, where a liquid feed can be included in the watering once a fortnight.

Above: Hand weeding is best in a border even when tackling a largish area. Use a fork to loosen the soil. Do not stand on the border when it is very wet or you will compact the structure of the soil.

Above: Planting close together will reduce the necessity for watering and weeding.

14

WEEDING

Try to do as much weeding as you can during drier spells in the winter and early spring. You can see the weeds at this time and they are generally easy to remove. A few minutes spent at this time of year saves hours later on. Always weed borders by hand. Never use chemicals on a planted border as there is always some drift on to other plants. Hoes can be used where there are large open spaces but it is surprising how often they seem to slip and cause damage. Besides, it is always best to get out all the roots of the weed. Once the growing season is in full swing, weed as often as necessary.

MULCHING

Applying a thick mulch – preferably at least 10cm (4in) – of well-rotted organic material such as manure, bark or

Above: *Potentillas look particularly attractive with a mulch of fine gravel.*

gravel, will help to retain moisture and also suppress weed germination. Always weed before mulching as existing weeds will grow through it, and always water thoroughly first if the ground is not already moist.

Above: *Mulching is very important and whether a border is newly planted, as here, or mature, it should receive a thick layer of organic material. Water and weed the ground before applying.*

15

STAKING

You may find that your plants need no staking if you choose short varieties or pack the plants close together, but most gardens contain at least a few plants that need to be staked. This is particularly true of gardens in exposed areas. There are several possible ways of staking.

1 There are various types of proprietary staking, such as this hoop or stakes that link together in various patterns, which can be used to secure plants. Put the staking in position while the plants are small. The plants will then grow up through the mesh. Adjust the height of the support so that it will come about halfway up the fully grown plants.

2 Pea-sticks (brushwood) are a cheap and renewable source of support. If foraging for your own, ensure they are not diseased. Push the sticks into the ground around the plant, being careful not to damage tender roots, and then bend over the tops to create a mesh.

3 Interweave or tie the bent-over tops of the sticks together so that they form a firm mesh through which the plants will grow. The mesh should be about halfway up the final height of the plants. The foliage will soon grow up and outwards, hiding the sticks.

4 For larger areas of plants use a mesh wire netting suspended on short stakes above the plants. Again, the plants will soon grow through the mesh, gaining support and at the same time hiding the wire.

5 Tall single-stemmed plants can be individually tied to stakes. Place the stake behind the plant so that it is hidden from view as much as possible. Add additional ties as the plant grows taller.

PERENNIALS
THAT NEED STAKING
Achillea
Campanula
Centaurea
Delphinium
Helenium
Paeonia
Papaver orientale
Sedum

Above: These daisies are well supported by staking, which is hardly visible beneath the mature plants.

DEADHEADING AND CUTTING BACK

Unless you want your plants to produce seeds, you can make them look neater by removing old flowerheads as they fade. This can involve cutting off just the heads or, in some cases, *Alchemilla mollis* for example, it is best to cut the whole plant to the ground. In the latter case, the foliage will grow anew and sometimes the plant will flower again. Once the plant begins to die back, it should be cut to the ground to await its regeneration in the following year. For the majority of perennials this is in the autumn. Some gardeners like to cut plants down straight away while others like to leave the dead stems throughout the winter, either because they look good or to provide seeds for birds and small mammals as well as refuges for insects. One problem with leaving them until the spring is that there is often so much to do at that time of year that everything is done in a rush, especially if a spell of bad weather prevents an early start.

PESTS AND DISEASES

Perennials are usually relatively robust and, while they do suffer from some pests and diseases, these are not generally a serious problem. A garden with a good mixture of plants tends to suffer far less than a monoculture. A variety of plants will help to attract beneficial insects that will predate on the more troublesome ones. Another factor is that pests tend to build up when there is plenty of food around and if there are only a few of each type of plant they rarely thrive. Good hygiene is also paramount. In cases of serious outbreaks where you do need to spray, do so with caution and only spray the affected parts.

Below: Geum 'Mrs J. Bradshaw' benefits from regular deadheading as it will flower over a longer period and look much tidier in the border.

Perennials in the Garden

THERE ARE COUNTLESS USES FOR PERENNIALS IN THE GARDEN. THEY CAN HELP TO CREATE A WIDE VARIETY OF STYLES, FROM THE FORMAL TO THE ROMANTIC. THEY ARE EQUALLY EFFECTIVE IN THE SMALL GARDEN OR IN THE WIDER SPACES OF A LARGE PLOT.

CONSIDERING YOUR SITE

As with most plants, it is best to grow perennials in sites where they will thrive rather than forcing them into situations where they will languish and probably die. This is not quite as serious as it may sound as most gardens provide areas that will grow a wide variety of plants. However, there are some things to think about. There is no point in growing sun-loving plants in the shade or shade-loving plants in the sun (some shade-loving plants will grow in the sun if the soil is moist enough). Some plants need a moist soil and will soon fade away in dry conditions, and vice versa.

So when considering the style of garden you want, do think about the conditions you can provide and how this will influence your choice. For example, very few silver foliage plants will grow in the shade. The best way to garden successfully is to work with nature and not against it. It may be possible to change the conditions – chop down a tree to let in more light or create a damp area in part of the garden, for example – but this will mean additional work.

Above: Using your own style and colour preferences will provide you with a garden that is uniquely yours and will be a source of inspiration for others.

CHOOSING A STYLE

The style of the garden is largely a matter of personal taste, as perennials will lend themselves to most designs. However, there may be a few restrictions. The site has already been mentioned. It is also important to consider the use of the garden as a whole. For example, if children are regularly playing in the garden, it may be difficult to maintain a formal border – an informal planting will be much more suitable. Similarly, a natural wildflower planting can look very out of place in a formal setting. However, in both these

cases, it may be possible to succeed with such a border if it is isolated, perhaps in its own area of the garden.

The gardener's personality is also important. It is inadvisable to consider having a neat formal border if you are a naturally untidy person who will soon let the border deteriorate. Similarly if your lifestyle is frenetic, with little time to spare, avoid complicated borders that are very time-consuming and perhaps choose something formal where maintenance may be minimal. Frequently style is dictated by needs. If you want to attract wildlife to your garden, then an informal style with plants that bear seeds or nectar will be important, as birds, bees and other beneficial insects rely on them for food.

Above: You will make a bold statement with a Mediterranean-style planting. There are plenty of plants to choose from and it can be very colourful.

Above: Aquilegia *and* Meconopsis cambrica *are more suited to an informal or cottage style garden where little maintenance is required. They will tolerate sun or light shade.*

HERBACEOUS BORDERS

These are the traditional ways of growing perennial plants. They consist of borders containing nothing other than herbaceous plants. They are usually planted in drifts, generally with the taller specimens at the back and shorter ones at the front. The colours are carefully planned so as to present a harmonious whole. The traditional colour scheme is hot, strong colours in the centre with cooler, softer ones at the ends. Some attractive herbaceous borders can be made by restricting the flowers to one colour, such as red, or perhaps two, such as white and gold or yellow and blue.

Perennials mostly look their best when they are set off against a green background, either shrubs or, better still, a yew hedge. Traditional herbaceous borders were long and often consisted of two parallel beds with a broad path between them. However, they can be of any shape you like to fit in either with your own designs or with the shape of your garden. Herbaceous borders can be quite labour-intensive but if you combine mulching with a "little and often" approach to maintenance, they are surprisingly easy to look after and are very rewarding. A wide range of plants, running to many thousands, are suitable.

Above: A herbaceous border on a grand scale, with two parallel beds separated by a wide path. With a careful choice of plants it can be kept attractive from spring to autumn.

Above: A mixed border of perennials and shrubs in early summer, planned to have plenty of colour later in the season.

Above: Island beds can be very effective in a larger garden. Create a path around them with grass, gravel or chipped bark.

MIXED BORDERS

Nowadays very few gardeners have herbaceous borders in the strictest sense. Most mix in a few other types of plants, such as roses and perhaps a few annuals. There is very little point in being a purist and sticking to one type of plant when the whole object is to create an attractive border. It makes sense to use whatever is available. A few shrubs will add a permanent structure to the border. The foliage of the shrubs can be used to set off the flowers of the plants in front of them. They can also provide a little shade for those plants that need it. In gardening terms there is very little difference between a mixed border and a herbaceous one. The shapes and design can be the same and apart from using other plants, aesthetically the two borders are likely to look very similar in style.

ISLAND BEDS

These are exactly the same as herbaceous and mixed beds except that they can be seen from all sides rather than from one or two. The main problem is that there is no background for the plants, so it makes sense to put taller plants in the middle, enabling the others to be seen against them. Shrubs or trees often make a good centre feature as they prevent the eye running straight over the bed to what lies beyond.

PERENNIALS FOR HERBACEOUS,
MIXED AND ISLAND BEDS

Achillea
Aster
Campanula
Delphinium
Geranium
Heliopsis
Nepeta
Paeonia
Rudbeckia
Solidago

COTTAGE STYLE

Traditional cottage gardens can be very attractive but they can also be a lot of work. Essentially they are borders with a profusion of old-fashioned flowers growing in them. Originally they had little structure with everything just planted where there were spaces, creating a joyous mixture of colour, shapes and sizes. Nowadays it is often more organized, with tall plants at the back and shorter ones at the front, and the colours planted a little more harmoniously. However well-organized, it should still represent a riot of colour. Self-sowing annuals are usually included with the perennials.

> COTTAGE GARDEN PERENNIALS
> *Alcea rosea*
> *Aquilegia vulgaris*
> *Aster*
> *Astrantia major*
> *Campanula persicifolia*
> *Dianthus* 'Mrs Sinkins'
> *Doronicum*
> *Geum rivale*
> *Lathyrus latifolius*
> *Lupinus* Russel hybrids summer
> *Primula vulgaris*
> *Salvia officinalis*

INFORMAL STYLE

Many gardeners prefer an informal style, especially if there are children who play in the garden. Here the perennials are used along with shrubs

Above: *A cottage garden, with a mixture of various types of flowers and plants spilling out in profusion over the path, gives an informal impression.*

and perhaps bulbs to create a colourful, comfortable background for family life. Small borders with tough plants that will stand a little neglect or the occasional football are what is required. Foliage plants are a good choice, as they have a long season and need little maintenance, along with colourful long-flowerers such as geraniums.

FORMAL STYLE

Creating a formal garden involves a layout with clean lines, often straight or with regular curves, such as circles. The planting is also regular, frequently using plants with clear lines and shapes, such as cordylines or yuccas, with their fountains of strap-shaped leaves. Edges may be tightly clipped box, lavender, or small, neat flowers. Repetition and symmetry are important. Small gardens are often ideal, especially if they are mostly paved.

WILDFLOWER GARDENS

An increasing number of gardeners are growing wildflowers to compensate for their loss in the countryside.

Below: A formal garden with repeated rhythms moving away from the house. The predominance of white and pink flowers helps to unify the garden.

This sounds simple, but can be as difficult as other types of garden. Wildflowers are best grown in a meadow or overgrown lawn, which should be mown regularly to avoid getting coarse grasses that will overpower the flowers. To start with, grow the flowers in pots and plant them into the meadow. These will establish more easily than if sown into the grass. Only grow wild plants that are appropriate to your area and soil.

PERENNIALS FOR A FORMAL GARDEN

Cordyline australis
Euphorbia characias
Iris
Miscanthus sinensis
Phormium tenax
Santolina pinnata subsp. *neapolitana*
Yucca gloriosa

Perennials for Different Conditions

ALL GARDENS HAVE A VARIETY OF DIFFERENT CONDITIONS IN WHICH TO GROW PLANTS. THERE ARE USUALLY AREAS OF SUN AND OTHERS OF SHADE. MANY GARDENS HAVE PONDS AND WITH THEM PATCHES OF RELATIVELY MOIST GROUND.

SUNNY AREAS

Most, but not all gardens have sun for at least part of the day. The majority of herbaceous plants will tolerate full sun. However, there are a number that will not and some that can only be grown in sun under special circumstances. Some plants that prefer shade, such as hostas, will grow in the sun if the soil is kept moist, but once it dries out they start to wilt. Others will grow in the sun but they should be protected from the really hot midday sun, violas being a good example. Some plants, especially those from

Above: Silver foliage plants need to grow in a sunny position. In the shade they will languish and eventually die. Here silver Stachys byzantina *is mixed with a sunloving* Nepeta.

Mediterranean climates, really thrive in hot, sunny conditions and are ideal for hot dry areas. These are particularly useful in areas that are close to house walls and receive little rain, or in gardens with light, dry soil. Most plants that need sunny conditions will not grow well in the shade.

Left: Grasses need a sunny position – very few of them will grow successfully in shade. When planted together they can make an interesting semi-formal planting.

24

SHADY AREAS

When planting in shady areas, the choice is slightly more limited than for sun, particularly with flowers, but so long as the soil is moist there are still a large number of suitable plants. Most of the flowering woodland plants flower in the spring, before the leaves appear on the trees – lily-of-the-valley and pulmonaria are good examples. However, there are still plenty of foliage and some flowering plants that will create a good display in the summer and into the autumn. If the area is dry, particularly under a large tree that takes a lot of moisture and nutrients from the soil, the choice is much more restricted. Some bulbous plants, such as anemones and cyclamen, are able to survive because they become dormant before the dryness of summer really sets in. Those plants that will tolerate dry shade, such as *Euphorbia amygdaloides* var. *robbiae* should be planted in drifts so that you will get maximum benefit from them.

Above: Geranium macrorrhizum *is one of the best shade plants, seen profusely flowering here in spite of being in quite dense shade. It will happily spread and form excellent ground cover.*

Creating Shade

If your garden is always sunny it is worth creating some shade just to enable you to grow a greater variety of plants. This can be achieved by planting trees or even large shrubs. Remove some of the lower branches so that light but not midday sun reaches the ground. A trellis screen covered with climbers, or perhaps a pergola or arch, will also provide some shade as well as creating an attractive feature. Keen gardeners often create shade beds by suspending netting on a framework above the bed. This is not very elegant but does allow you to extend your range of plants and also gives you time to establish a tree.

**FLOWERING PERENNIALS
FOR SHADE**

*Anemone nemorosa
Brunnera macrophylla
Convallaria majalis
Eranthis hyemalis
Euphorbia amygdaloides* var. *robbiae
Helleborus viridis
Lamium galeobdolon
Lathyrus vernus
Liriope muscari
Polygonatum
Sanguinaria canadensis
Smilacina
Trillium*

WATERSIDE AREAS

There are a large number of perennials that will grow in water or in the mud surrounding it. These tend to be specialist plants that will only grow in these conditions. Waterside planting can add another dimension to the garden. Because they have a plentiful supply of water, the plants' foliage tends to stay fresh for most of the year, often creating an oasis in an otherwise dry garden. The colours are predominantly yellow and blue, but most other colours can be found, allowing an attractive planting scheme to be developed. The main problem with water plants is that many of them can be invasive. These will need to be reduced every so often, or planted in bottomless pots in the ground, to allow the more delicate plants to survive.

PERENNIAL WATERSIDE PLANTS

Aruncus dioicus
Astilbe x *arendsii*
Caltha palustris
Cardamine pratensis
Gunnera manicata
Iris ensata
Lobelia cardinalis
Lythrum salicaria
Onoclea sensibilis
Persicaria bistorta
Primula japonica
Rodgersia pinnata

MOIST AREAS

Many people with ponds also have a damp area next to them in which to grow the wide range of plants that like a moist but not waterlogged situation. Other gardeners deliberately create such an area as they want to grow moisture-loving plants but cannot have a pond for safety reasons. Such areas, often called bog gardens,

Above: Primulas and many irises are ideal plants for a streamside position.

26

Above: The arum lily can be planted either in shallow water or in marshy margins. It can also be used in a bog garden.

can be a very attractive feature. Many of the plants are colourful and some, such as gunnera, can grow very large, creating eye-catching features.

Dry Areas

Areas with light, free-draining soil can become very dry in summer, particularly when they also receive a lot of sun. Mediterranean-type plants love these conditions. However, many gardens with light soil will still become very wet in the winter, because of higher rainfall than occurs in the Mediterranean climate, which can be a problem for these plants. There are still many plants that can tolerate these conditions, but it is a good idea to increase the moisture-retentiveness by adding plenty of organic material to the soil, and also mulching. This will enable you to grow a wider range of plants.

Mediterranean Beds

In recent times Mediterranean-style beds have become very popular. A lot of gravel is added to the borders, so that they drain very quickly, preventing the plants becoming waterlogged in winter. This type of bed is ideal for very dry climates. A wide range of plants can be grown, and the beds can look very attractive and require little maintenance.

PLANTS FOR A DRY GARDEN
Allium hollandicum
Cistus purpurea
Cordyline australis
Euphorbia characias subsp. *wulfenii*
Lavandula angustifolia
Ophiopogon planiscapus 'Nigrescens'
Papaver somniferum
Rosmarinus
Salvia nemorosa 'Superba'
Sedum
Stachys byzantina
Verbascum

Above: A small, sunny courtyard can be an ideal site for Mediterranean garden plants that tolerate dry conditions.

27

PERENNIALS IN CONTAINERS

As well as using conventional beds, it is possible to grow perennials in containers of various types. Not all perennials will grow in containers – Michaelmas daisies, for example, really need to be planted in the ground. However, there are many perennials that are suitable. Foliage plants such as hostas work very well in containers, as do several of the more architectural plants. Cordylines and yuccas, for example, can look very impressive when planted in an attractive container.

Above: The soft mauve trumpets of Convolvulus sabatius *work well in this warm terracotta pot. This is a tender perennial and a smaller pot makes it easier to move into shelter for the winter.*

Above: A young ruby cordyline recently planted in a deep terracotta pot with the silver-leaved Lotus berthelotti *as a foil. These will soon grow into substantial plants to make a focal point in the garden.*

Choosing Containers

On the whole, perennials should be grown in large containers. Generally window boxes and hanging baskets are too small, as there is no room for root development. This is not important with annuals but is crucial for perennials, which often do not flower until they have established themselves in their second year. Large ceramic pots or wooden tubs or boxes are best. There are a few plants that can be grown in smaller containers, such as violas and diascias, but these will usually need replacing at regular intervals.

Siting Containers

You can place your filled container anywhere in the garden, but they are particularly useful on patios or paved areas where there are no beds. If possible use a grouping of pots. Either combine different sizes of container or stand some of the pots on bricks to vary the height of the group. In larger gardens, pots of perennials look particularly eye-catching placed on either side of a flight of steps or a gateway. Ends of paths make another excellent location. Some of the more statuesque plants, such as cordylines, when used in containers can make good focal points at the end of vistas or pathways.

Planting Techniques

Perennials can be planted in the same way as any other plants in containers, but it is a good idea to use a loam-based compost (soil mix) for longer plantings, as the nutrients will not be exhausted so quickly, as with standard potting compost. It is important that there are some drainage holes in the container. Place a layer of drainage material in the bottom of the container and fill with compost. Put the plant into it and firm down the compost, topping up with more if necessary so that its final level is just beneath the rim. Water thoroughly. When planting, make sure the plants have plenty of room to grow or they will quickly need potting on to a larger container.

Above: The colour and shape of the pot should be chosen to suit the plant.

PERENNIALS FOR CONTAINERS

Agapanthus
Begonia x *tuberhybrida*
Cordyline
Dianthus
Diascia
Euphorbia
Hemerocallis
Heuchera
Nepeta
Oenothera fruticosa subsp. *glauca*
Phormium tenax
Yucca

Maintaining Containers

The main thing to remember with containers of perennials is that they need regular watering. In hot weather, this can often be more than once a day. With this regular passage of water through the compost the nutrients are washed out and so they need regular replacement, either with a liquid feed every two weeks or by adding a slow-release fertilizer to the compost.

Choosing Perennials with Special Qualities

WITH SUCH A LARGE RANGE OF PERENNIALS AVAILABLE TO THE GARDENER IT IS NOT SURPRISING THAT MANY HAVE INTERESTING FEATURES THAT CAN BE USED IN A VARIETY OF DIFFERENT WAYS, EITHER INDIVIDUALLY OR MIXED WITH OTHER PLANTS.

FRAGRANT PERENNIALS

Many perennials have a smell of one kind or another. Some are delightfully sweet, such as dianthus, others are rank and foetid; *Dracunculus vulgaris*, for example. As always there is an in-between group, represented by such plants as *Phuopsis stylosa*, the smell of which some people find attractive and others repulsive. One tends to think

Above: *Phlox has an intoxicating fragrance from mid- to late summer. It is ideal for the back of a border.*

of fragrance in terms of flowers, but many plants have fragrant foliage and this can be an important element in the garden. However, it is the flowers that most people love the best, particularly those that fill the whole area around them with fragrance. Lily-of-the-valley *(Convallaria majalis)* is one such plant, and it will rapidly spread to form large drifts, producing an intoxicating scent.

Above: *Popular lily-of-the-valley is one of the few fragrant perennials that will flower in the shade.*

Aromatic Foliage

Most aromatic foliage needs to be crushed or at least brushed before it issues its scent. One of the best scents is that of monarda, which releases a wonderful fragrance at the slightest touch. If possible plant them near a path where they can be touched or brushed against.

Scent for Different Times

Fortunately, not all flowers are scented at the same time. Surprisingly, a large number of winter-flowering plants – *Iris unguicularis*, for example – are highly scented, probably because they need to attract pollinating insects and there are not many around in winter. Spring is also good, but it is the height of summer when the warm weather brings out the greatest number of perfumes. Plants also vary in their scents during the course of the day, many reserving their smell for the evening to attract the night-flying moths. *Cestrum parqui* is a curiosity as it has a savoury smell during the day, probably to attract flies, and a sweet scent in the evening to attract moths.

Using Scents

While a scented garden provides a great deal of pleasure and sensuous stimulation, mixing too many scents together is self-defeating, as you end up smelling none of them. It is better to spread the scents out so that you come

Above: Nepeta *has the advantage of scented leaves and attractive flowers.*

on them one at a time. Areas where you sit and relax are good places for scented flowers. Beds near the house where fragrance can waft through open windows can also be delightful.

SCENTED PERENNIALS
FLOWERS
Alyssum maritinum
Cestrum parqui
Convallaria majalis
Cosmos atrosanguineus
Dianthus
Erysimum cheiri
Filipendula ulmaria
Iris
Mirabilis jalapa
Phlox
Viola odorata
FOLIAGE
Agastache foeniculum
Anthemis punctata subsp. *cupaniana*
Melittis melissophylum
Monarda
Morina longifolia
Nepeta
Salvia

CLIMBING PERENNIALS

There are a small number of climbing perennials that add variety to the range of plants when you are planning your border. However, with the exception of golden hop, *Humulus lupulus* 'Aureus', they are generally not as vigorous as many of their shrubby counterparts. They are relatively short growing but this can make them ideal for inclusion in the herbaceous or mixed borders. Climbing perennials are treated in exactly the same way as ordinary perennials. Some are self-clinging or twining and will even attach themselves to their supports, but others will need to be tied in.

Supporting Climbers

Some climbers, such as a selection of the violas and geraniums, are scrambling plants rather than true climbing

Above: This viola and thrift are growing through a rose.

plants and are extremely useful for growing through the base of low bushes. Others, and here many of the geraniums such as 'Ann Folkard' or 'Salome' are perfect, will happily scramble across other plants, often providing colour when their host plant has finished flowering. If you choose carefully you can extend the flowering period considerably.

The true climbers can also be draped over other plants, but they are best supported in some other way. The majority, being relatively low growing, can be used in the border supported by wigwams of twiggy sticks to create attractive mounds of colour. The golden hop, being vigorous, may be used in a more conventional climbing way. It can be trained to grow over pergolas or arches, or up poles.

Above: The golden hop is a perfect plant for growing over an arch or pergola.

Herbaceous Clematis

Most clematis are shrubby but there are just a few that are herbaceous in character and die back each autumn. These tend not to be tall climbers but are well worth considering both for foliage colour (*Clematis recta* 'Purpurea') and for their flowers (*C. durandii*). Again, twiggy sticks form the best kind of support.

> ### PERENNIAL CLIMBERS
> *Clematis erecta*
> *Eccremocarpus scaber*
> *Humulus lupulus* 'Aureus'
> *Lathyrus*
> *Solanum dulcamara* 'Variegatum'
> *Tropaeolum speciosum*
> *Vinca major*

GROUND COVER

There are generally two main reasons for using ground-cover plants: either to suppress weeds, or to provide a low-maintenance covering for an area where not many types of plants will thrive, such as a shady area or a bank. In the latter case the ground cover may also help prevent soil erosion. Either way, perennials are perfect. Virtually any perennial, if planted close enough together, will form ground cover, the basic requirement for weed suppression being that the foliage prevents light reaching the soil. Some make better cover than others as their foliage is dense or large, creating shade. Hostas are a prime example.

Suppressing Weeds

If the plants are covering the ground effectively, any weed seeds that germinate will quickly die from lack of light. However, ground cover will not suppress perennial weeds if their roots are already in the soil. For this reason it is

Above: Persicaria affinis *makes a dense carpet of foliage that is the perfect weed-suppressing ground cover.*

vital to remove all perennial weeds before planting the ground cover. Otherwise, they can be difficult to eradicate without digging up the whole bed.

> ### PERENNIALS FOR GROUND COVER
> *Acaena*
> *Anthemis punctata cupaniana*
> *Bergenia*
> *Epimedium*
> *Geranium macrorrhizum*
> *Hosta*
> *Pulmonaria*
> *Stachys byzantina*
> *Vinca minor*

FOLIAGE PERENNIALS

Among the perennials are some truly delightful foliage plants. Some are used purely as foliage plants, either not producing flowers or having all the flowers removed as these spoil the effect. Others are ordinary flowering plants but they also have very good foliage. This attribute is rather useful when the plant is flowering as well as before and after flowering. *Alchemilla mollis* is a good example.

Above: *Silver foliage has a softening effect in a border. Two popular species are* Stachys *and* Artemisia.

The Qualities of Foliage

Foliage is attractive for several different reasons. Although the majority of perennials have green foliage there is also a wide range of other colours, including variegation where more than one colour is present. Then there are the size and shape, which can vary from thin strap-like leaves to huge rounded ones. The texture is also important. Shiny leaves, for example, are useful

Above: *These rodgersias have a wonderful ribbed texture that contrasts well with the smoothness of the water. The fans of leaves also complement the foliage of the iris.*

FOLIAGE AND ARCHITECTURAL PERENNIALS

FOLIAGE
Canna
Cordyline
Cynara
Grasses
Gunnera manicata
Hosta
Rheum
Rodgersia
Stachys byzantina

ARCHITECTURAL
Acanthus spinosus
Angelica archangelica
Cortaderia selloana
Cynara cardunculus
Gunnera manicata
Phormium tenax
Rheum
Stipa gigantea

for illuminating dark areas. Light and shade play an important part in the use of foliage. Foliage plants can simply be used as a foil for other plants, or they can be decorative in their own right, either among flowering plants or in a purely foliage border. Mixing foliage with contrasting characteristics always creates interesting designs. It can also be used as a break between two plants with flower colours that do not quite go together visually, so that they do not jar on the eye.

ARCHITECTURAL PLANTS

There are some plants with a striking, statuesque shape that immediately draws the eye, foliage generally being the most important element. *Gunnera manicata*, for example, has large eye-catching leaves, while cordyline has narrow leaves arranged in such a beautiful way that they cannot but attract attention. These plants will act as focal points in the garden, and this should be remembered when planning the design. They may be used at the end of a straight path or at a bend in a curved one. The feature may be away in the distance at the end of a lawn or on the boundary of the garden. Often this attraction accentuates the length of a path or of a garden, making it look bigger than it is. Architectural plants can also be effective in a border, perhaps in the middle or at regular intervals to set up a rhythm, which is particularly useful in a formal setting.

Above: Gunnera manicata *has some of the largest leaves of any garden perennial. A clump of these certainly creates an imposing sight.*

35

Perennials for Colour

OF ALL THE QUALITIES OF PERENNIALS, COLOUR IS PROBABLY THE
MOST IMPORTANT. IT IS THE FIRST THING MOST PEOPLE NOTICE
ABOUT A PLANT AND IT GENERALLY MAKES THE MOST IMPACT. THE
ART OF CHOOSING COLOUR IS EXPLAINED BELOW.

USING COLOUR

You can make a perfectly acceptable
flower garden without worrying
about colour theory at all. Most of the
old cottage gardeners had no idea
about such things and yet they produced some of the most gloriously
colourful gardens, purely by instinct.
So there is no reason why you could
not do the same. However, it does
help to have some idea of how to use
colour because in the long run the
results are much more satisfying.

THE COLOUR WHEEL

Colours tend to either harmonize or
contrast. When colours harmonize they
are easy on the eye; they are pleasant
to look at and create a feeling of
gentle wellbeing. Colours that contrast
are much more lively and sometimes
disturbing. On the artist's colour wheel,
colours that harmonize are next to
each other and those that contrast are
on opposite sides. Thus orange and
blue are contrasting colours but blue
and purple are harmonizing colours.

Above: *This striking yellow grass,*
Milium effusum *'Aureum', is an effective
companion for the pale yellow primulas.*

Above: *This pink phlox has been well set
off by the silver foliage of the* Anaphalis
planted in front of it.

COLOUR WHEEL

Artists and gardeners have long been aware that colours have a relationship to each other and that these can be displayed in a simple wheel. On the wheel adjacent colours, blue and purple for instance, combine in a sympathetic way and are easy on the eye.

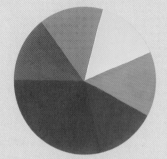

Colours on opposite sides of the wheel, such as blue and orange, are contrasting colours and tend to jar and shock the eye. Both have their uses in creating a border.

PURPLE PERENNIALS

Aster (various)
Echinacea purpurea
Erigeron 'Dunkelste Aller'
Erysimum 'Bowles Mauve'
Geranium (various)
Lythrum
Osteospermum jucundum
Penstemon 'Burgundy'
Phlox 'Le Mahdi'
Primula denticulata
Senecio pulcher
Verbena bonariensis

Combining Purple and Violet

Blues and mauves can combine beautifully with purple and violet, and a few pinks will also add life. White makes a more startling contrast, softened if the white is tinged with pink. Purple flowers can look very striking against lime green foliage. Plants with purple foliage can set off many colours, particularly red and orange.

PURPLE AND VIOLET

Violet is a deep blue with a touch of red in it. This red gives the blue a rich, vibrant quality. It is a much warmer blue than the pure blues. If yet more red is added then it becomes purple. These are strong dependable colours that often have a rich velvety quality about them. They speak of luxury. A border containing such plants tends to have substance. However, these colours used in quantity can become a bit heavy and rather leaden and a whole border devoted to them can become boring as the eye searches for some light relief.

Above: *Opposite colours on the colour wheel, in this case orange and blue, combine to striking effect.*

BLUE

This is a wonderful cool colour that has a freshness about it. Many spring flowers are blue, which contributes to the vitality of that season. There are few really true blues, but anyone who grows gentians or anchusas will have seen blue at its piercing best. These deep blues can really take the breath away. Paler blues, as in some of the campanulas or veronicas, are more misty in their effect and are pleasant to the eye rather than intense. A border devoted almost entirely to blues, with an emphasis on deep blues, can be very attractive.

Above: Campanulas provide some of the best blues in the perennial garden, varying from the softest of tones through to rich violet hues.

Softer Blue

There is a whole range of softer blues, sometimes with touches of pink in them which bring the blue towards lavender and mauve. These have an ethereal quality about them. They are useful for creating misty designs that have a romantic, airy look. These colours can often be bleached out by bright sunlight, but in greyer, more overcast climates they really come into their own. There is something particularly magical about plants such as scabious, which have relatively small flowerheads on long wiry stems. Mixed with other such delicate plants they can create a summery haze of soft colours. Other soft or pastel colours, such as pinks or creams, can also look very effective in this type of planting.

Mixing Blues

Orange is the complementary or contrasting colour to blue. If the two colours are mixed together they can make a startling combination. This works well but should not be overplayed or the border will become too restless for the eye and will lose its attraction. Yellow is a near complementary colour and this also generally works well with blue. Both are fresh colours, and when they are combined their freshness seems to be enhanced. A whole border devoted to blue and yellow can create a delightful effect.

In the Shade

The paler blues can show up beautifully in a shady position, and can almost seem to glow with an ethereal, ghostly quality in the fading evening light. If you like to sit in the garden in the evening, plant some blue flowers such as aquilegia or campanula in the area where you sit; if you also have some scented flowers nearby, it will be heaven on a warm evening.

Above: The soft blue of Eryngium *blends well with the creamy flowers of* Santolina.

BLUE AND VIOLET PERENNIALS
Agapanthus
Ajuga reptans
Aquilegia flabellata
Baptisia australis
Campanula
Delphinium
Echinops ritro
Eryngium
Gentiana
Iris
Limonium platyphyllum
Nepeta
Perovskia atriplicifolia
Scabiosa
Veronica

Above: *The globe-shaped flowerheads of* Echinops *are a beautiful soft blue, darker in the centre.*

39

YELLOW

In contrast to the cooler blue, yellow is a wonderfully vibrant and lively colour. You only have to think of sunshine to appreciate its cheerfulness. A garden with yellows in it can never be dull. It is very much the colour of spring when everything is fresh. Many of the flowers are yellow and even the green foliage is flushed with it. It is the sign of renewal and regeneration. It also appears at the other end of the year and is one of the main colours of the autumn, both in flowers and foliage. The colour is more mellow at this time, in the slanting autumn light.

Yellow tends to have two sides to its character. When it is mixed with blue, it takes on a greenish tinge and has a cool, fresh character. On the other hand there are those yellows that have a little red

Above: The intense yellow of Lysimachia, together with the fresh green foliage, creates a vibrant, sunny feel.

added, and these have a more golden or orange hue, which feels warmer. Both aspects are widely represented in the garden, as well as pure yellow, which is often mixed with a little white to give shades of primrose and cream.

Above: A superb drift of flat-topped achilleas adds dignity and calmness to a border as well as striking colour.

YELLOW PERENNIALS

Achillea
Anthemis tinctoria
Asphodeline lutea
Helenium
Helianthus
Hemerocallis
Lysimachia punctata
Oenothera
Trollius
Verbascum

Mixing Yellows

Yellows are very versatile and will mix with most other colours. The softer colours go very well with other pastel shades to make a hazy, romantic image that is redolent of summer days. The stronger, warmer yellows fit in well with the hot reds and the oranges. They create a bright and very vibrant effect and can be used to create entire hot-coloured borders. Yellows can be extremely attractive when seen against green, especially the dark green of a yew hedge. They also contrast well with bright blues. Unlike the softer blues, which produce a hazy effect, yellow and bright blue create a crisp, fresh look.

ORANGE

This is a much hotter colour than yellow, as it is moving towards red. It has a strong personality and makes much of its position, often clashing with other colours. Being close to red, it has a lively quality that brightens up a border. It is not a plant to use if you want tranquillity and softness.

Above: *Lychnis x 'Arkwrightii' has intensely orange flowers that are well set off against its dark purple foliage and stems.*

Mixing Oranges

Orange goes best with the other hot colours, the reds and the golden yellows. Mixing these together creates an intensely lively border with lots of drama. However, you will not want to overdo it. A border composed of these colours is fine but a whole garden of them would be very restless and ultimately boring as the eye would need some respite.

The hot character of orange can be tempered by mixing it with cream flowers or with a bronze foliage.

ORANGE PERENNIALS

Canna 'Orange Perfection'
Crocosmia
Dahlia
Gazania
Geum 'Borisii'
Kniphofia
Potentilla 'William Rollison'

RED

Very few colours stir the emotions as red does. It stands for danger and for excitement. There is little danger from this colour in the garden but there can be plenty of excitement. Red is also a complex colour. As with so many other colours there are two sides to its nature. One is when it has orange in its make-up. These are the fiery reds. The other is when it includes blues. These are much more subdued and smouldering colours, especially when they lean towards purple.

The Fiery Reds

This group comprises the vermilions and scarlets, the colours of flames. These are the true live wires of the border. They can be used to inject a feeling of drama, or they can be combined with other hot colours such as the golds and oranges to create a border devoted to hot colours. This will be full of activity, but if you are not careful it can be overdone. A little is exciting; too much becomes draining. The eye gets very tired as these are restless colours and provide it with nowhere to linger.

The Blue Reds

These reds, based around crimson, can also be very bright but they can be more comforting colours. They are dramatic without being overexciting and have a more sedate quality than the fiery reds, especially as they move

Above: Kniphofia 'Red Admiral' is *appropriately erect and brightly coloured.*

Above: Spirited red dahlias and crocosmias stand out in a lively border.

Above: Zauschneria californica *display a riot of small red flowers that are offset by their soft grey-green foliage.*

towards purple. These will not mix comfortably with the orange reds but combine more happily with purples, violets and blues. They will also go well with pinks.

Drawing the Eye

One quality that the bright reds, especially the fiery ones, have is that they draw the eye. If you place a clump of red flowers in a border they will immediately be noticed. This can be useful if you want to create a focal point. Such reds also seem to be closer than they really are and if flowers are placed at the end of a long border the border will appear to be shorter. All reds, but especially the fiery ones, can look fabulous against green foliage such as hedges.

RED PERENNIALS
Alcea Rosea
Astilbe 'Fanal'
Astrantia major 'Ruby Wedding'
Canna
Centranthus ruber
Cosmos atrosanguineus
Dahlia
Dianthus 'Brympton Red'
Geum 'Mrs Bradshaw'
Hemerocallis 'Stafford'
Lobelia 'Cherry ripe'
Lupinus 'Inverewe Red'
Lychnis chalcedonica
Monarda didyma 'Cambridge Scarlet'
Paeonia
Papaver orientale
Penstemon 'Cherry Ripe'
Persicaria amplexicaulis
Potentilla 'Gibson's Scarlet'
Zinnia

PINK

This is a warm colour with a wide range of different flower shades ranging from white just tinged with pink to vivid carmine or magenta, almost into purple. As with other colours, there are two extremes of pink. There are those based on the fiery reds which are mixed with yellow and white to produce the peachy and apricot pinks, and those where white has been added to the blue reds to produce the soft bluey pinks. As so often happens the two types do not sit happily if they are grown together. Pinks occur at all times of the year but are most common in summer and the pale pinks can be blanched by bright sunlight to look even paler.

Peachy Pinks

These are a delightful collection of colours. Frequently the colour is not totally mixed but the petals will exhibit both pink and yellow coloration, especially when they are in bud. They can be used in a general mixture of colours without causing any disruption, or they can be mixed with related colours.

Peachy pinks are warm colours, and some will go well with yellows, oranges and even reds, although some of the brighter reds and oranges may be too overpowering. The softer varieties also go well with pastel colours and can be used to create a soft romantic border where colours float and mingle.

Above: *A wonderful combination of pinks with the spires of* Linaria 'Canon Went' *and the globes of* Allium christophii.

Bluey Pinks

These include the bright magentas and carmines. They are cooler than the peachy pinks and work much better with the purples and blues. The brighter ones, the magentas, are not always easy to place in a border. They will often blend in more easily if placed with silver foliage, to tone down the brightness. The paler ones are relatively easy and will mix with any of the purples, blues, mauves and whites. However, they do not combine happily with reds.

Above: Geraniums provide some of the best pink flowers in the garden. Some only have a short flowering season but there are many that will flower all summer.

Avoid Blandness

Although it can be fun to create an all-pink border, it could become a bit bland if you went as far as to fill the garden with pink flowers. It is important to get the balance right and to introduce some brighter colours to draw the eye and to create interest.

PINK PERENNIALS

Anemone x hybrida
Aster
Astilbe
Bergenia cordifolia
Dianthus
Diascia
Dicentra
Erodium manescaui
Geranium
Lamium roseum
Linaria purpurea 'Canon Went'
Malva moschata
Monarda didyma 'Croftway Pink'
Papaver orientale 'Cedric Morris'
Penstemon 'Hidcote Pink'
Persicaria
Phlox
Phuopsis stylosa
Primula
Sedum
Sidalcea

Above: This pink Penstemon *'Pennington Gem' will add grace to the border.*

45

WHITE

This is the colour of purity and tranquillity. In the garden, both of these aspects often come into play, especially when the whole border or garden is restricted to white. It is a very useful colour in the garden as it will combine with most other colours. It works equally well under bright, sunny skies or dull grey ones. White is a clear-cut colour, especially when seen against green backgrounds, and it is perfect for bringing out the shape of a flower. Compare, for example, white aquilegias with those of another colour and notice the distinction. The white flowers of *Crambe cordifolia* float in a way that no other colour could hope to imitate. This clarity is one reason why white gardens work so well: the shapes of the flowers are more noticeable and so add interest along with the colour.

In the Shade

White flowers shine out especially well in dark corners, and will illuminate the gloom. These plants are also extremely attractive in the early evening as the light fades. They do not have quite the luminosity of blue, but the white stands out strikingly in the fading light, eventually becoming ghostlike. Plant them where they can be seen at this time of the evening.

White Borders

These are the most popular of all single-coloured borders, and it is not difficult to see why. As long as care is taken when mixing the subtly different shades of white, there are no jarring colours and a peaceful, restful effect is produced. In fact, the interest depends largely on the shape of the flowers, and the colours and qualities

Above: Planting Arabis alpina *subsp.* caucasica 'Flore Pleno' *against a purple-leaved shrub enhances the white blooms.*

Above: Achillea ptarmica 'The Pearl' *produces an abundant display of pure, almost luminous white flowers.*

Above: A mixture of white-flowered perennials is nearly always beautiful. The contrasts are produced by the variation in flower shape and the foliage.

WHITE AND CREAM PERENNIALS

WHITE

Achillea ptarmica 'The Pearl'
Anemone x hybrida 'Honorine Jobert'
Anthemis punctata subsp. *cupaniana*
Campanula lactiflora alba
Convallaria majalis
Crambe cordifolia
Dicentra spectabilis 'Alba'
Geranium
Gypsophila
Penstemon
Phlox
Polygonatum hybridum
Silene uniflora
Trillium grandiflorum
Zantedeschia aethiopica

CREAM

Anemone lipsiensis
Aruncus dioicus
Kniphofia 'Little Maid'
Rodgersia
Sisyrinchium striatum
Smilacina racemosa
Trollius 'Alabaster'

of the foliage. Actually "white garden" in some ways is a misnomer as it does not take into account the greens, greys and blues of the foliage. Green hedges, especially yew, are a particularly good foil for white borders or gardens as they make the white seem purer and more intense.

Off-whites

Slight touches of other colours can be added to white to produce very subtly coloured whites. Creams have a touch of yellow and blush pinks a hint of pink. These colours are all well represented by flowers. White flowers will mix with most other coloured flowers, as we have seen, but off-whites can make a less contrasting combination. Thus creams can work well with yellows and blush pinks with pinks.

Seasonal Splendour

MANY PERENNIALS FLOWER FOR RELATIVELY SHORT PERIODS, AND THOUGH THIS CAN SOMETIMES SEEM A DRAWBACK, IT DOES GUARANTEE A CONSTANTLY CHANGING PICTURE. BY CAREFULLY PLANNING YOUR PLANTING, YOU CAN ENSURE INTEREST THROUGHOUT THE YEAR.

SPRING

This is the season of birth and renewal. It is the time when barren earth suddenly springs into life in a myriad of colours, each with its own kind of freshness. The predominant colours are yellow and blue, but all the other colours are also present. It is not only the flowers that are exciting and new; it is also the foliage, which appears in a seemingly limitless number of shades of green.

Planting for Spring

A good way to plan your spring planting is to choose those colours that represent the freshness and vitality of the season, such as yellow primroses, blue anemones and red pulmonarias. The silver-spotted foliage of the pulmonarias will continue to look attractive for a long time, but most of the spring-flowering perennials add little to the scene once they have finished flowering.

Above: Spring is a wonderful time of year with many old favourites, such as primulas, aquilegias and forget-me-nots, coming into flower.

SPRING PERENNIALS
Aubrieta deltoidea
Bergenia cordifolia
Caltha palustris
Doronicum 'Miss Mason'
Euphorbia polychroma
Helleborus orientalis
Primula vulgaris
Pulmonaria angustifolia
Sanguinaria canadensis
Smilacina racemosa
Trollius europaeus
Viola odorata

Above: An important perennial in any spring garden is Euphorbia polychroma, *which forms a perfect dome of gold up to 75cm (30in) high.*

Indeed many, such as the anemones, die back below ground and are not visible. Plant these types of flowers towards the back of the border or between other plants where they will show up in spring when the shoots are only just beginning to appear, but will be hidden when the later plants are fully grown.

No special maintenance is required for spring perennials except to remove any dead foliage as it appears. Try to weed and mulch the borders before too much growth has been made to avoid damaging the plants.

Woodland Plants

Many spring plants are of woodland origin, and appear, flower, seed and die back before the trees come into leaf. This allows them to make full use of the available light and moisture. Anemones and celandines are of this type. In the garden, they can be planted under deciduous shrubs and trees, where later-flowering plants would not

thrive because of the shade created by the foliage. Some perennials that keep their foliage, such as primroses, hellebores and pulmonarias, can also be used in such places.

Above: The soft greyish pink of this dicentra is unusual in spring.

49

EARLY SUMMER

At this time, the spring-like quality of freshness is still in evidence in the garden, and yet the multitude of colours and abundance of lush vegetation give a decidedly summery feel. As yet the sun is usually not too strong and so the colours have a brightness and intensity that they lose as summer progresses. Spring is colourful, but this colour is mainly seen against bare earth. By early summer the foliage has nearly all developed and the flowers are viewed against a wide range of foliage colours and shapes, which enhances them considerably.

Above: *Early summer would not be complete without the towering spires of blue produced by delphiniums.*

Planting for Early Summer

The plants for early summer seem to be quite distinct from those later in the summer. In a late season many are left over from spring and the two periods can merge, with dicentras lasting into summer and *Geranium pratense* starting in spring. Although it is a good idea to try to co-ordinate the colours in the border, do not place all the early-flowering plants together or there will be gaps later in the year when they die; try to spread them among the later-flowering plants.

Long-lasting Plantings

Some plants have modern hybrids that flower for longer than the older varieties. For example, old-fashioned pinks tend to flower only once, in early summer, whereas many of the modern pinks, although not so attractive to many people and often less fragrant, do flower throughout the whole summer and well into autumn. Some plants that start to flower in early summer, such as the Mexican daisy, *Erigeron karvinskianus,* or *Erodium manescaui* continue to flower profusely throughout the whole summer and often until the first frosts appear. Some plants that do not flower for very long can be used as foliage plants for the later part of the summer. Either cut them back to the ground and let them regenerate, as you can with alchemilla, or remove the flowering heads, for example with lupins. Some

plants, such as *Alchemilla mollis* and delphiniums, may well flower again later in the year if cut back.

Early Summer Maintenance

In the initial part of early summer, while the plants are still putting on lots of growth, be certain to stake

Above: Alchemilla mollis *often flower twice if cut back in mid-season.*

Above: There are many perennial wallflowers, which are valuable for their cheerful colours in the early summer.

them. If this is done now, the plants will hide the staking under the new foliage. Deadhead as plants go over. If the borders have been properly mulched there should be no need to water, but if there is a prolonged dry spell it may become necessary.

EARLY-SUMMER PERENNIALS

Alchemilla mollis
Baptisia australis
Campanula persicifolia
Centaurea montana
Delphinium
Dianthus 'Mrs Sinkins'
Geranium pratense
Hemerocallis
Lupinus Russell hybrids
Papaver orientale

51

HIGH SUMMER

The borders in high summer can be drenched in sunshine. Some of the brighter colours, such as the reds, still stand out but many of the others have lost the freshness of early summer and are subdued into a haze. It can be one of the best times in the garden, but so often things begin to flag and steps should be taken to overcome this.

Summer Colours

To create a border that retains its colour at this time of year, it is best to use hot reds or oranges, such as some of the kniphofias and heleniums. White also holds up well in this light, especially if seen against green. Most of the soft pastel colours are bleached even paler by the bright light, but with hazy, romantic borders the effect can be enhanced – perfect for lazy summer days.

Flagging Foliage

Much of the foliage has been around since spring and it is beginning to look tired and ragged. Try to offset this by cutting back plants that have finished flowering earlier in the year, so that they produce fresh leaves to brighten up the borders. Regular deadheading will also help to keep the borders looking neat. Mulching should have helped to keep the moisture in the soil, but in a hot summer reserves may be used up and it may be necessary to water copiously until the ground is again fully saturated and the plants are revived.

Above: Helenium 'Indian Summer' brings an orange glow with its sun-loving flowers.

52

Above: Lillies are always popular for their attractive blooms and range of colours.

Beside the Water

By midsummer the water in the ponds has warmed up and the water plants are in full growth. This is one of the fresher-looking parts of the garden, both in the water and along its margins. Water lilies and irises are at their best and the colours are still vibrant. In dry gardens, where this time of year may be a problem, it is worth creating a water feature to provide an oasis of fresh greenery and colourful flowers.

The Importance of Planning

In the spring and early summer enthusiasm for gardening is high, and along with this the tendency to buy and plant out new plants. However, one's eye is often caught by plants that are in flower rather than ones yet to flower. This can easily upset the balance of plants in the garden with a preponderance of plants for spring and early summer and far less for high summer. Try to be forward-looking and plan for this period too.

FLOWERS FOR HIGH SUMMER
Acanthus
Astilbe
Campanula
Dianthus
Eryngium
Geranium
Helenium
Hemerocallis
Kniphofia
Lilium
Phlox
Veronica

Above: Different yellows with soft pink astilbes make a lovely summer border.

53

AUTUMN

As autumn sets in, nature begins to wind down, but with good planning this can be one of the most colourful times of the year in the garden. By now, many plants are usually looking decidedly the worse for wear, but with judicious cutting back it should be possible to remove the more unsightly plants and dead flowers so that the autumn colours have a chance to shine through. A lot of the end-of-season look that many gardens have during this time of year can be avoided simply by cutting out spent material.

Autumn Colours

This season is a time of warm and hot colours with many yellow daisies, such as helianthus and rudbeckias, as well as fiery autumn foliage. However, there are still plenty of other colours. The Michaelmas daisies, in particular,

Above: Michaelmas daisies are among the stars of the autumn garden. They come in a wide variety of colours.

produce a wide range of colours including blues, pinks and whites. Vernonias also have some wonderfully rich purples as well as whites.

Moving Plants

One of the problems with perennial gardening is to manage to accommodate enough plants in a border to maintain a continuous supply of colour from flowers and foliage. By mid-autumn many of the plants have finished, leaving large gaps in the arrangements. This is not so much a problem at other times of the year as there are always plants in leaf, although they may not yet be in flower. One solution is to move some plants. This works well with shallow-rooted plants, of which Michaelmas

Above: Rich gold is one of the prime colours of the autumn scene and long-flowering rudbeckias provide it.

AUTUMN-FLOWERING PERENNIALS

Anemone x hybrida
Aster
Boltonia
Chelone
Chrysanthemum
Helianthus
Kirengeshoma
Liriope
Nerine
Ophiopogon
Rudbeckia
Schizostylis
Sedum
Solidago
Tricyrtis

Above: A number of sedums flower in the autumn and these are not only valuable for their colour but also for the way that they attract butterflies and bees.

daisies are the prime candidates. Surprisingly these can be moved in full flower without any detrimental effect. Grow them in a spare bit of ground or the back of the border. Soak them well as they come into flower. Dig up the clump with a good rootball of soil still attached, replant it in a gap in the border and then water again. This is real instant gardening.

Wildlife

Autumn is a wonderful time for butterflies, moths and bees in the garden. Fortunately there are plenty of plants, such as the sedums and the Michaelmas daisies, that provide food for these visitors. It is worth making certain that you grow several attractant plants, as the sight of these creatures adds another dimension to the garden. If you want to provide winter food and shelter for birds and insects then you should leave

some areas of herbaceous material such as seed heads for them to feed on during the winter, although this may mean that the garden looks less neat and tidy than it would otherwise.

Above: The dainty flowers of Schizostylis *appear in the autumn. They come in a range of reds and pinks.*

55

WINTER

This is the most difficult time of year in the garden. And yet in some ways it can be the most interesting as it certainly is a challenge. The weather can vary dramatically from region to region and in some areas there may be total snow cover throughout the darkest months, in which case the main interest in the garden will be trees and shrubs. On the other hand there are mild areas that can support a surprisingly large range of material. In the middle are those that have a mildish winter with a few cold snaps here and there. Where the ground can be seen, as long as it is not frozen or waterlogged, there are always a number of plants to be grown.

Above: Iris reticulata *gives a warming splash of colour in late winter.*

Winter Flowers

There are only a handful of perennials that flower in the winter but combined with other plants, such as bulbs and shrubs, they can make up a good display. Some of the most popular winter plants are the hellebores. There are a number of species and an ever-increasing number of cultivars in a wide range of colours. The foliage of many species is very attractive and the plants are worth growing for this alone. Another worthwhile winter perennial is the winter iris, *I. unguicularis*. This flowers over a long period, throughout most of the dullest months. It has wonderful soft blue or mauve flowers that have a delightful scent. It has one other advantage in that it can be grown in the poorest of soils. Indeed an ideal spot is in a dry, rubble-filled soil next to a wall.

Surprise Appearances

If you are not in too much of a hurry to cut everything to the ground in autumn, it is surprising how many plants can continue to flower if the weather is mild, right into the middle of winter and beyond. Penstemons are good examples of this long- and late-flowering ability. Similarly in a mild winter many of the spring flowers will flower early. Sweet violets, *Viola odorata*, are usually flowering in winter, as are a number of primroses and ground-covering pulmonarias.

Where to Plant

Because winter flowers are generally not very interesting for the rest of the gardening year, they can be planted towards the back of the border or under deciduous shrubs where they will clearly show up in the winter but be covered by other plants when they are not looking at their best. If you have a large garden and can afford the space you might create a special winter garden, which you only visit at this time of the year.

ALL-YEAR-ROUND PLANTS

Some perennials have all-year-round qualities that make them especially useful if you have limited space. Although pulmonarias have their

Above: The appearance of winter aconites is a welcome sign as it shows that winter will soon be over.

flowers in late winter and spring, they can be used as a foliage plant for the rest of the year. If all the foliage is cut back after flowering, new leaves will quickly regrow and will retain their freshness. Bergenias have spikes of pink, red or white flowers in spring, but, again, retain their attractive leaves for the rest of the year.

Above: The unusual, delicate pale green flowers of these hellebores brighten up the garden in the winter.

WINTER-FLOWERING PERENNIALS
Eranthis hyemalis
Euphorbia rigida
Galanthus
Helleborus niger
Helleborus orientalis
Helleborus purpurascens
Iris ungicularis
Primula vulgaris
Pulmonaria rubra
Viola odorata

Best Perennials for Your Garden

Use this quick reference chart to select the plants most suitable for your design and garden conditions. Unless otherwise stated, all plants should be sown or planted out in the spring (or autumn in milder areas).

Plant Name	Height/Spread	Colour/Period of Interest	Method of Propagation
Acanthus	150cm (5ft)	white and purple/summer	seed
Achillea	120cm (4ft)	yellow, white, pink/summer	division
Actaea	180cm (6ft)	white/summer and autumn	seed or division
Agapanthus	90cm (3ft)	blue, white/summer	division
Alchemilla	38cm (15in)	yellowish green/summer	seed
Allium B	90cm (3ft)	all colours/summer	seed or division
Alstroemeria	90cm (3ft)	all colours/summer	division
Anemone	90cm (3ft)	white, blue, pink, yellow/spring	autumn division
Anthemis	75cm (30in)	white, yellow/summer	cuttings or division
Aquilegia	60cm (2ft)	all colours/spring, early summer	seed
Artemisia	120cm (4ft)	yellow, brown/silver foliage/summer	cuttings or division
Aruncus	2m (7ft)	cream/summer	division
Aster	2m (7ft)	all colours/summer and autumn	division
Astilbe	120cm (4ft)	white, pink, red/summer	division
Astrantia ps	60cm (2ft)	greenish, pink, red/late spring, summer	division
Bergenia fs or ps	45cm (18in)	pink/evergreen foliage/spring	division
Caltha ms	45cm (18in)	yellow/summer	seed or division
Campanula	120cm (4ft)	blue, white/summer	seed or division
Canna	150cm (5ft)	Red, pink, yellow/summer and autumn	division
Cardiocrinum s B	3m (10ft)	white/summer	seed or division
Catananche	45cm (18in)	blue/summer	seed
Centaurea	120cm (4ft)	purple, red, pink, yellow/summer	seed or division
Centranthus	75cm (30in)	reddish pink, white/summer	seed
Cephalaria	2m (7ft)	yellow/summer	seed
Chelone	90cm (3ft)	pink/autumn	division
Chrysanthemum	180cm (6ft)	various colours/autumn	cuttings or division
Clematis	180cm (6ft)	blue, white/summer	cuttings

Above: Crocosmia '*Lucifer*'

Above: Geranium sanguineum '*Album*'

Convallaria S	20cm (10in)	white/late spring	division
Coreopsis	75cm (30in)	yellow/summer into autumn	division
Cortaderia G	2.5m (8ft)	various colours/all year round	division
Cosmos S	45cm (18in)	mahogany/summer	cuttings or division
Crambe S	180cm (6ft)	white/early summer	division
Crinum B	120cm (4ft)	pink/late summer	seed or division
Crocosmia B	120cm (4ft)	orange, red, yellow/late summer	division
Cynara	2.5m (8ft)	purple/silver foliage/late summer	division
Dahlia T	120cm (4ft)	various colours/summer into autumn	division or cuttings
Delphinium	2m (7ft)	blue, pink, white/summer	cuttings, division or seed
Dianthus S	Up to 38cm (15in)	pink, white/summer	cuttings
Diascia	38cm (15in)	pink/summer into autumn	cuttings
Dicentra	75cm (30in)	pink, white/late spring into early summer	division
Dictamnus	90cm (3ft)	purple, white/summer	seed
Dierama	150cm (5ft)	pink/summer	seed or division
Digitalis	180cm (6ft)	purple, yellow, brown/summer	seed
Doronicum	90cm (3ft)	yellow/spring	division
Echinacea	150cm (5ft)	summer	division
Echinops	180cm (6ft)	blue, white/summer	seed
Epimedium ps	45cm (18in)	yellow, white, pink/late spring	division
Eremurus	2m (7ft)	pink, yellow/summer	seed or division
Erigeron	60cm (2ft)	purple, blue, pink, white/summer	division
Eryngium	2m (7ft)	blue, green/good foliage/summer	seed or division
Eupatorium	2m (7ft)	pink, white/summer and autumn	division
Euphorbia	150cm (5ft)	yellowish-green/spring into summer	seed or division
Filipendula S	120cm (4ft)	pink, white/summer	division
Foeniculum	2m (7ft)	yellow/good, fragrant foliage/summer	seed
Francoa	75cm (30in)	pink/summer	seed
Fritillaria B	90cm (3ft)	various colours/spring	seed or division
Gaura	90cm (3ft)	white/summer	seed
Gentiana	90cm (3ft)	blue, white, yellow/summer and autumn	seed or division
Geranium	90cm (3ft)	purple, pink, blue, white/spring into autumn	seed, cuttings or division
Geum	45cm (18in)	red, yellow, pink/spring into summer	division
Gladiolus B	120cm (4ft)	in various colours/summer	division
Gunnera	2.5m (8ft)	green/large foliage/summer	division
Gypsophila	120cm (4ft)	white, pink/summer	seed or cuttings
Helenium	150cm (5ft)	yellow, orange, brown/summer	division

Above: Anemome ranunculoides

Above: Gypsophila paniculata

Helianthus	2.5m (8ft)	yellow/summer into autumn	division
Heliopsis	150cm (5ft)	yellow/summer into autumn	division
Helleborus	60cm (2ft)	various colours/winter into spring	seed or division
Hemerocallis	120cm (4ft)	yellow, orange, red, pink/summer	division
Heuchera	90cm (3ft)	white, pink/good foliage/summer	division
Hosta	60cm (2ft)	blue, white/good foliage/summer	division
Humulus C	6m (20ft)	green/good foliage/summer	division
Inula	2.5m (8ft)	yellow/summer	seed or division
Iris	150cm (5ft)	various colours/summer, winter	division
Kirengeshoma ps	90cm (3ft)	yellow/autumn	seed or division
Knautia	75cm (30in)	crimson, pink/summer	division, cuttings or seed
Kniphofia	180cm (6ft)	red, orange, yellow/summer into autumn	division
Lamium	60cm (2ft)	pink, purple, white/good foliage/summer	cuttings or division
Lathyrus C	120cm (4ft)	various colours/spring into summer	seed or division
Ligularia	180cm (6ft)	yellow/summer into autumn	seed or division
Lilium some S	180cm (6ft)	various colours/summer	seed or division
Limonium	90cm (3ft)	blue/summer	seed or division
Linaria	180cm (6ft)	yellow, purple, pink/summer	seed
Linum	45cm (18in)	blue/summer	seed
Liriope	38cm (15in)	purple/autumn	division
Lobelia	150cm (5ft)	various colours/summer into autumn	cuttings, division or seed
Lupinus S	150cm (5ft)	various colours/early summer	seed or cuttings
Lychnis	75cm (30in)	red, cerise, pink, orange/summer	seed
Lysimachia	120cm (4ft)	yellow, white, red/summer	seed or division
Lythrum	120cm (4ft)	purple/summer	cuttings or division
Macleaya	2m (7ft)	pink, white/summer	root cuttings or division
Meconopsis	150cm (5ft)	blue, yellow, white, red/summer	seed or division
Miscanthus G	2.5m (8ft)	various/all year round	division
Monarda SF	150cm (5ft)	red, pink, purple, white/summer	division
Nepeta SF	150cm (5ft)	mauve, blue, white, and yellow/summer	cuttings or division
Nerine B	45cm (18in)	pink/autumn	division
Oenothera	150cm (5ft)	yellow, orange/summer into autumn	seed
Origanum SF H	45cm (18in)	purple/summer	seed or division
Osteospermum	Up to 38cm (15in)	purple, white/summer	cuttings
Paeonia	75cm (30in)	red, pink, white, yellow/spring into summer	seed or division
Papaver	75cm (30in)	various colours/summer	seed or division
Pennisetum G	90cm (3ft)	various colours/all year round	seed or division

Above: Rheum

Above: Astrantia major

Penstemon	90cm (3ft)	various colours/summer	cuttings
Perovskia	120cm (4ft)	blue/summer	cuttings
Persicaria	120cm (4ft)	pink, white/summer	division
Phlox	120cm (4ft)	in various colours/summer	cuttings or division
Phormium	180cm (6ft)	red, green/good foliage/summer	division
Physostegia	90cm (3ft)	pink, white/summer	seed or division
Polemonium	90cm (3ft)	blue, white, pink, yellow/summer	seed or division
Polygonatum ps	90cm (3ft)	white/spring into summer	division
Potentilla	60cm (2ft)	red, yellow/summer	division
Primula	60cm (2ft)	in various colours/winter/summer	seed or division
Pulmonaria ps	30cm (12in)	blue, red, white/some good foliage/ late winter into spring	division
Rodgersia	120cm (4ft)	pink, cream/good foliage/summer	division
Rudbeckia (cone)	2m (7ft)	yellow/summer into autumn	division
Salvia	150cm (5ft)	in various colours/summer into autumn	cuttings or division
Scabiosa	75cm (30in)	lilac, pink, yellow/summer	seed or division
Schizostylis B	60cm (2ft)	pink, crimson/autumn	division
Sedum	60cm (2ft)	pink, red, yellow/summer	cuttings
Sidalcea	120cm (4ft)	pink, white/summer	division
Silene	60cm (2ft)	pink, white/spring into summer	seed or division
Sisyrinchium	60cm (2ft)	yellow, blue, white, purple/summer	seed or division
Stachys	60cm (2ft)	purple, pink, yellow/silver foliage/summer	some division
Stipa G	2m (7ft)	various colours/all year round	division
Thalictrum	180cm (6ft)	various colours/summer	seed
Tradescantia	60cm (2ft)	blue, purple, white/summer	division
Trillium ps	45cm (18in)	various colours/spring	seed or division
Trollius ms	75cm (30in)	yellow, orange/spring into summer	seed or division
Veratrum	180cm (6ft)	green, red/summer	division
Verbascum	180cm (6ft)	yellow, pink, white/summer	seed
Verbena	180cm (6ft)	purple, blue/summer	seed or division
Veronica	120cm (4ft)	blue, pink, white/summer	division
Viola	30cm (12in)	various colours /summer	cuttings
Yucca	2m (7ft)	cream/summer into autumn	division
Zantedeschia ms	90cm (3ft)	white/summer	division

KEY TO SYMBOLS

fs = full sun	s = shade	H = herb	SF = scented foliage
ms = moist soil	B = bulbous	G = grasses	T = tuberous
ps = partial shade	C = climber	S = scented	

Above: Lathyrus latifolius

Above: Aquilegia

Common Names of Plants

Where the common name and the botanical name are the same, as with chrysanthemums, dahlias, delphiniums and gypsophila, the plants are not listed here. Increasingly, old common names are being dropped in favour of botanical names, thus *Hosta* tends to be known as hostas rather than plantain lilies.

African lily *Agapanthus*
arum lilies *Zantedeschia*
avens *Geum*
bear's breeches *Acanthus*
bellflower *Campanula*
bergamot *Monarda*
betony *Stachys*
blazing star *Liatris*
bridal wreath *Francoa*
burnet *Sanguisorba*
buttercup *Ranunculus*
calamint *Calamintha*
Californian poppy *Romneya*
campion *Silene*
cape figwort *Phygelius*
cardoon *Cynara*
catchfly *Lychnis*

Above: *A subtle Mediterranean planting.*

catmint *Nepeta*
columbine *Aquilegia*
comfrey *Symphytum*
coneflower *Rudbeckia*
coral flower *Heuchera*
day lily *Hemerocallis*
deadnettle *Lamium*
dittany *Dictamnus*
elephant's ears *Bergenia*
evening primroses *Oenothera*
feather grass *Stipa*
fennel *Foeniculum*
flax *Linum*
fleabane *Erigeron*
foxglove *Digitalis*
fritillary *Fritillaria*
gay feather *Liatris*
gentian *Gentiana*
globe flowers *Trollius*
globe thistle *Echinops*
golden rod *Solidago*
hardy geranium *Geranium*

hellebore *Helleborus*
hemp agrimony *Eupatorium*
Himalayan poppy *Meconopsis*
hop *Humulus*
ice plants *Sedum*
ironweed *Vernonia*
Jacob's ladder *Polemonium*
Kaffir lily *Schizostylis*
king cup *Caltha*
knapweed *Centaurea*
knotweed *Persicaria*
lady's mantle *Alchemilla*
leopard's bane *Doronicum*
lily *Lilium*
lily-of-the-valley *Convallaria*
loosestrife *Lysimachia*
lungwort *Pulmonaria*
lupin *Lupinus*
mallow *Malva*
marsh marigold *Caltha*
masterwort *Astrantia*
meadow sweet *Filipendula m*

Michaelmas daisy *Aster*
mint *Mentha*
money flower *Mimulus*
monkshood *Aconitum*
montbretia *Crocosmia*
mulleins *Verbascum*
New Zealand flax *Phormium*
ornamental onion *Allium*
ox eye *Heliopsis*
pampas grass *Cortaderia*
sweet peas *Lathyrus*
peony *Paeonia*
Peruvian lily *Alstroemeria*
pinks *Dianthus*
plantain lily *Hosta*
plumbago *Ceratostigma*
poppy *Papaver*
purple loosestrife *Lythrum*
purple cone flower *Echinacea*
red-hot poker *Kniphofia*
Russian sage *Perovskia*
scabious *Scabiosa*
sea holly *Eryngium*
Sneezeweed *Helenium*
Solomon's seal *Polygonatum*
speedwells *Veronica*
spurge *Euphorbia*
statice *Limonium*
stonecrops *Sedum*
sunflower *Helianthus*
toadflax *Linaria*
torch lily *Kniphofia*
tree mallow *Lavatera*
turflily *Liriope*
turtle's head *Chelone*
wake robin *Trillium*
windflower *Anemone*
wormwood *Artemisia*
yarrow *Achillea*

Index

Above: Convolvulus sabatius.

Index

Above: Hemerocallis.